MASSACHUSETTS

Julie Murray

Big Buddy BOOKS
Explore the United States

VISIT US AT
www.abdopublishing.com

Published by ABDO Publishing Company, PO Box 398166, Minneapolis, MN 55439.

Copyright © 2013 by Abdo Consulting Group, Inc. International copyrights reserved in all countries. No part of this book may be reproduced in any form without written permission from the publisher. Big Buddy Books™ is a trademark and logo of ABDO Publishing Company.

Printed in the United States of America, North Mankato, Minnesota.
042012
092012

 PRINTED ON RECYCLED PAPER

Coordinating Series Editor: Rochelle Baltzer
Editor: Sarah Tieck
Contributing Editors: Megan M. Gunderson, BreAnn Rumsch, Marcia Zappa
Graphic Design: Adam Craven
Cover Photograph: *Shutterstock*: Pierdelune.
Interior Photographs/Illustrations: *Alamy*: Everett Collection Inc (p. 13); *AP Photo*: AP Photo (p. 25), Stew Milne (p. 21), North Wind Picture Archives via AP Images (pp. 13, 23); *Getty Images*: Photo Researchers (p. 30); *iStockphoto*: ©iStockphoto.com/burwellphotography (p. 27), ©iStockphoto.com/kickstand (p. 26), ©iStockphoto.com/SOMATUSCANI (p. 27), ©iStockphoto.com/DenisTangneyJr (pp. 11, 27, 29), ©iStockphoto.com/ThereseMcK (p. 30), ©iStockphoto.com/KenWiedemann (pp. 19, 26); *Shutterstock*: Steve Byland (p. 30), Steve Heap (p. 17), jiawangkun (p. 9), Phillip Lange (p. 30), Jim Lozouski (p. 5), Stephen Orsillo (p. 9).

All population figures taken from the 2010 US census.

Library of Congress Cataloging-in-Publication Data

Murray, Julie, 1969-
  Massachusetts / Julie Murray.
    p. cm. -- (Explore the United States)
  ISBN 978-1-61783-359-5
  1. Massachusetts--Juvenile literature. I. Title.
  F64.3.M87 2012
  974.4--dc23
                        2012007058

Contents

ONE NATION

The United States is a **diverse** country. It has farmland, cities, coasts, and mountains. Its people come from many different backgrounds. And, its history covers more than 200 years.

Today the country includes 50 states. Massachusetts is one of these states. Let's learn more about this state and its story!

Did You Know?

Massachusetts became a state on February 6, 1788. It was the sixth state to join the nation.

Massachusetts is part of New England. This area of the United States is known for having beautiful fall colors.

5

Massachusetts Up Close

The United States has four main **regions**. Massachusetts is in the Northeast.

Massachusetts shares borders with five states. New Hampshire and Vermont are north. New York is west. Connecticut and Rhode Island are south. The Atlantic Ocean is east.

Massachusetts has a total area of 8,262 square miles (21,398 sq km). About 6.5 million people live there.

Did You Know?

Washington DC is the US capital city. Puerto Rico is a US commonwealth. This means it is governed by its own people.

REGIONS OF THE UNITED STATES

= West
= Midwest
= South
= Northeast

CANADA

WASHINGTON
MONTANA
OREGON
IDAHO
WYOMING
NEVADA
UTAH
CALIFORNIA
COLORADO
ARIZONA
NEW MEXICO

NORTH DAKOTA
MINNESOTA
SOUTH DAKOTA
WISCONSIN
NEBRASKA
IOWA
KANSAS
MISSOURI
OKLAHOMA
ARKANSAS
TEXAS

MICHIGAN
ILLINOIS
INDIANA
OHIO
KENTUCKY
TENNESSEE
MISSISSIPPI
LOUISIANA
ALABAMA
GEORGIA
FLORIDA

VERMONT
MAINE
NEW HAMPSHIRE
MASSACHUSETTS
NEW YORK
RHODE ISLAND
CONNECTICUT
PENNSYLVANIA
NEW JERSEY
Washington DC ★
DELAWARE
WEST VIRGINIA
MARYLAND
VIRGINIA
NORTH CAROLINA
SOUTH CAROLINA

PACIFIC OCEAN
ATLANTIC OCEAN

ALASKA

MEXICO

GULF OF MEXICO

HAWAII

PUERTO RICO

N
W E
S

7

IMPORTANT CITIES

Boston is the **capital** of Massachusetts. It is also the state's largest city, with 617,594 people. Boston is a busy seaport. It is on Massachusetts Bay.

Boston is known for its history. The Boston Tea Party took place there in 1773. This important event helped lead to the **Revolutionary War**.

Did You Know?

Boston's nickname is "Beantown." This comes from colonial times. Back then, beans baked in molasses became a popular dish there.

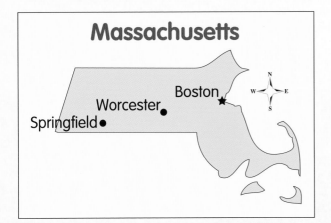

Massachusetts

Springfield • Worcester • Boston ★

★★★★★★★★★★★★★★★★★★★★★★★★★★★

The Old State House is one of Boston's historic buildings. It was built in 1713.

★★★★★★★★★★★★★★★★★★★★★★★★★★★

The Public Garden is a large park in Boston. It has a statue of George Washington, the first US president.

Worcester (WUS-tuhr) is the second-largest city in Massachusetts. It has 181,045 people. This city is on the Blackstone River. In the spring, many rowing teams race on nearby Lake Quinsigamond.

Springfield is the third-largest city in the state. It is home to 153,060 people. It is known as the birthplace of basketball. The Naismith Memorial Basketball Hall of Fame is located there.

Worcester has hospitals, colleges, and factories.

Springfield is on the Connecticut River.

11

Massachusetts In History

The history of Massachusetts includes Native Americans, colonists, and war. Native Americans have lived in present-day Massachusetts for thousands of years.

In 1620, the Pilgrims landed in Plymouth and formed a settlement. The Massachusetts Bay Colony began in 1629. In 1775, the **Revolutionary War** started there. Colonists won their freedom from England in 1783. Five years later, Massachusetts became the sixth state.

The Pilgrims sailed from England on the *Mayflower*.

★ **Did You Know?**

The settlement in Plymouth was one of the earliest permanent settlements in the United States.

Native Americans taught the Pilgrims how to hunt, fish, and farm. In 1621, the Pilgrims shared their food with them. This was the first Thanksgiving.

Timeline

1776

1716

1788

Boston Light was built. It was the first US lighthouse.

Colonists fought against England's soldiers at the Battles of Lexington and Concord. This was the start of the **Revolutionary War**.

Massachusetts became the sixth state on February 6.

1700s

1800s

Colonists dumped 342 chests of tea into Boston Harbor. They did this to oppose England's rule over them. This was called the Boston Tea Party.

John Adams of Braintree became the second US president.

John Quincy Adams of Braintree became the sixth US president. He was the son of John Adams.

1797

1825

1773

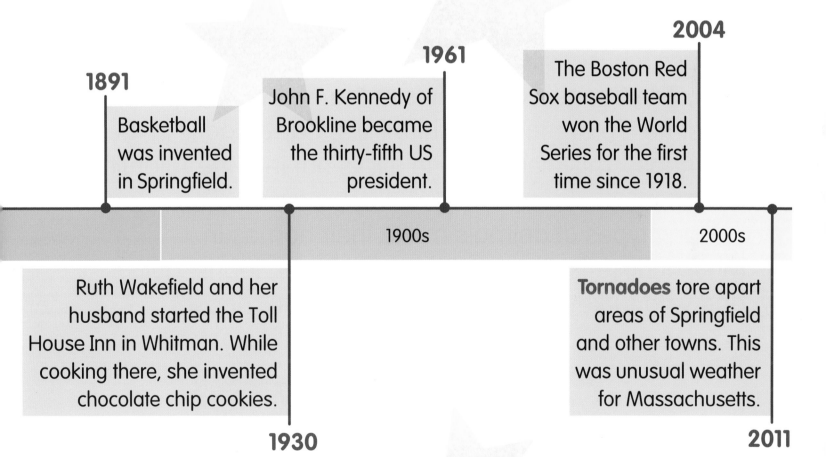

1891

Basketball was invented in Springfield.

1961

John F. Kennedy of Brookline became the thirty-fifth US president.

2004

The Boston Red Sox baseball team won the World Series for the first time since 1918.

1900s

2000s

Ruth Wakefield and her husband started the Toll House Inn in Whitman. While cooking there, she invented chocolate chip cookies.

Tornadoes tore apart areas of Springfield and other towns. This was unusual weather for Massachusetts.

1930

2011

ACROSS THE LAND

Massachusetts has forests, coasts, and rolling, open land. The Connecticut River is in the western part of the state. So are the Berkshire Hills. Cape Cod is in the southeast. This piece of land sticks out into the Atlantic Ocean.

Many types of animals make their homes in Massachusetts. These include red foxes, loons, gulls, and wild turkeys. Sometimes people see moose!

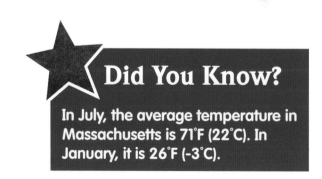
Did You Know?

In July, the average temperature in Massachusetts is 71°F (22°C). In January, it is 26°F (-3°C).

Bash Bish Falls is in the Berkshire Hills.

17

EARNING A LIVING

For hundreds of years, Massachusetts has been a shipping and fishing state. Its farmers produce dairy products and plants. Today, it also has a lot of **technology** businesses. And, many people have jobs helping visitors to the state.

Massachusetts is known as a medical and educational center. Some people work in the state's famous hospitals and colleges. Harvard University, Wellesley College, and Boston College are well known.

Cranberries are an important crop in Massachusetts.

19

SPORTS PAGE

Many people think of sports when they think of Massachusetts. That's because the state is home to popular baseball, basketball, football, and hockey teams.

This state also hosts the Boston Marathon. It is the oldest footrace in the United States. It has been held every year since 1897. People come from around the world to race.

Did You Know?

The New England Patriots are a famous football team in the state. They won the Super Bowl in 2001, 2003, and 2004.

Every April, thousands of people run in the Boston Marathon.

HOMETOWN HEROES

Many famous people are from Massachusetts. Benjamin Franklin was born in Boston in 1706. Franklin was a printer, an inventor, and a scientist.

Franklin helped make the United States a country. He signed the **Declaration of Independence**. He also helped create the first US city hospital.

Franklin helped write the Declaration of Independence.

Franklin flew a kite outside during a thunderstorm. This helped him learn about lightning and electricity.

John F. Kennedy was born in Brookline in 1917. He became the thirty-fifth US president in 1961.

President Kennedy was known as a strong leader. As president, he solved problems between the United States and the Soviet Union. He also supported African Americans during the **civil rights movement**. Sadly, he was **assassinated** on November 22, 1963.

Kennedy was the youngest person ever elected US president. He was 43 years old when he took office.

Tour Book

Do you want to go to Massachusetts? If you visit the state, here are some places to go and things to do!

 ## Remember

Visit the town of Salem to learn about its history. In 1692, many people there were put on trial for witchcraft. Today, you can see historic buildings from this time.

 ## Play

Spend time on Cape Cod in the summer. You can hike, bike, hunt for seashells, and swim in the Atlantic Ocean.

 # Explore

Walk through the grounds of Harvard University in Cambridge. Founded in 1636, it is the oldest college in the United States!

 # Taste

Try some Boston baked beans at a local restaurant. They are made by cooking beans in molasses.

 # Walk

Follow the Freedom Trail through historic Boston. You'll see old government houses, churches, and the home of Revolutionary War hero Paul Revere. The trail ends at the famous USS *Constitution* (*left*).

A GREAT STATE

The story of Massachusetts is important to the United States. The people and places that make up this state offer something special to the country. Together with all the states, Massachusetts helps make the United States great.

Cape Cod features beaches, sand
dunes, woodlands, and ponds.

29

Fast Facts

Date of Statehood:
February 6, 1788

Population (rank):
6,547,629
(14th most-populated state)

Total Area (rank):
8,262 square miles
(45th largest state)

Motto:
"Ense Petit Placidam Sub
Libertate Quietem" (By the
Sword We Seek Peace, But
Peace Only Under Liberty)

Nickname:
Bay State, Old Colony State

State Capital:
Boston

Flag:

Flower: Mayflower

Postal Abbreviation:
MA

Tree: American Elm

Bird: Black-Capped
Chickadee

Important Words

assassinate to murder an important person by a surprise or secret attack.

capital a city where government leaders meet.

civil rights movement the public fight for civil rights for all citizens. Civil rights include the right to vote and freedom of speech.

Declaration of Independence a very important paper in American history. It announces the separation of the American colonies from Great Britain.

diverse made up of things that are different from each other.

region a large part of a country that is different from other parts.

Revolutionary War a war fought between England and the North American colonies from 1775 to 1783.

technology (tehk-NAH-luh-jee) the use of science for practical purposes.

tornado a strong wind with a funnel-shaped cloud. A tornado moves in a narrow path.

Web Sites

To learn more about Massachusetts, visit ABDO Publishing Company online. Web sites about Massachusetts are featured on our Book Links page. These links are routinely monitored and updated to provide the most current information available.

www.abdopublishing.com

Index